WE GOT GAME!

WE GOT GAME!

35 FEMALE ATHLETES
WHO CHANGED THE WORLD

by **Aileen Weintraub**
Illustrations by **Sarah Green**

RP|KIDS
PHILADELPHIA

Running Press Kids
Hachette Book Group
1290 Avenue of the Americas, New York, NY 10104
www.runningpress.com/rpkids
@RP_Kids

Printed in China

First Edition: May 2021

Published by Running Press Kids, an imprint of Perseus Books, LLC, a subsidiary of
Hachette Book Group, Inc. The Running Press Kids name and logo is a trademark
of the Hachette Book Group.

The Hachette Speakers Bureau provides a wide range of authors for speaking events.
To find out more, go to www.hachettespeakersbureau.com or call (866) 376-6591.

The publisher is not responsible for websites (or their content)
that are not owned by the publisher.

Print book cover and interior design by Marissa Raybuck
Interior and cover illustrations by Sarah Green

Library of Congress Control Number: 2020930996

ISBNs: 978-0-7624-9780-5 (hardcover), 978-0-7624-9781-2 (ebook)

1010

10 9 8 7 6 5 4 3 2 1

TO REMINGTON

CONTENTS

INTRODUCTION

Do you play sports? Maybe you dream about scoring a goal on the soccer field, hitting a home run in softball, shooting a three-pointer on the basketball court, or landing a triple axel on the ice in front of a cheering crowd. Perhaps you're thinking about trying a new sport, but you're not sure.

In this book you'll meet female athletes who played hard, broke records, and inspired kids around the world. Some of these athletes played years ago. Others are still competing. But they all have one thing in common: they all **Got Game!**

You'll read about the first female horse jockey to compete in the Kentucky Derby, the number one tennis player in the world, a surfer who lost her arm in a shark attack, and a snowboarder who landed a death-defying jump, as well as many more. Not only are these amazing women world-class champions, they are using their fame and success to help others in a big way. The athletes in this book fight for gender equality, raise awareness about the challenges people with disabilities face, promote body positivity, work to end cyberbullying, find new ways to protect the environment, and so much more!

These women have shown true sportsmanship, both on and off the field, ice, court, and wherever else they play. Just like them, you can achieve anything you set your mind to, whether it's becoming an Olympic swimmer, a ballerina, or even a mountaineer.

Are you ready to be inspired? Let's find out how these fascinating female athletes are making the world a better place.

WE GOT GAME!

SIMONE BILES

GREATEST GYMNAST OF ALL TIME, BORN 1997

AMAZING FACTS AND UNBELIEVABLE STATS

SIMONE'S INTEREST IN GYMNASTICS

BEGAN AT AGE SIX

ON A FIELD TRIP.

...

THE ASSOCIATED PRESS NAMED HER

2019 FEMALE ATHLETE

OF THE YEAR,

MAKING HER THE FIRST GYMNAST
TO WIN THE AWARD TWICE.

...

SHE IS AN OLYMPIC

GOLD MEDALIST

IN VAULT, FLOOR, INDIVIDUAL,
AND TEAM ALL AROUND.

Simone Biles held her breath. It was the moment she had been waiting for her whole life. She was fourteen years old and trying out for the USA Gymnastics women's artistic junior team. The results were in: Simone didn't make the cut. She was convinced it was the end of her career. Little did she know it was only the beginning.

She continued to practice, and a year later, Simone won first place all around at the US Classic, a competition for elite female artistic gymnasts in the United States. The following year, she became the first African American to win the All-Around Champion title. She also became famous for her now signature move known as The Biles: a double twist with a half flip and a front-facing landing on the floor exercise. She won the All-Around Champion title four more times, making her the first gymnast in history to earn the title of five-time World All-Around Champion.

Simone was unstoppable. In 2016, she qualified for the US Olympic team nicknamed The Final Five. She became the first US female gymnast to win four gold medals at a single Olympic Games. Two years later, she won all five events at the US National Championships. At the 2019 championships, she became the first gymnast in history to land a double-twisting double somersault from the balance beam. Then, during the floor exercise, she wowed the world again by landing a record-setting triple-twisting double somersault. After this amazing performance, people began calling her the GOAT—the Greatest of All Time.

As of 2021, Simone holds six national titles, has racked up twenty All-Around victories in a row, and has earned twenty-five World Championship medals, nineteen of them gold! She is the most decorated American gymnast in history! *Time* magazine called her one of the most influential people in the world.

But life for Simone hasn't always been easy. She spent her early years in foster care until her grandparents adopted her and her sister. That's why she now brings attention to the needs of children in foster care. She talks about her own experiences and the importance of making sure children have proper homes. She set up a scholarship fund for foster kids and others, and has also teamed up with Mattress Firm Foster Kids to donate clothing and school supplies.

When her medical records were released without her permission, it was discovered that she had a disability called attention deficit/hyperactivity disorder (ADHD). She began talking about ADHD and how she treats it with medication. As one of the most famous athletes in the world, Simone inspires her fans to dream big!

GRETCHEN BLEILER

EXPERT SNOWBOARDER, BORN 1981

AMAGING FACTS AND UNBELIEVABLE STATS

WHEN GRETCHEN LANDED
THE CRIPPLER 540,
SHE CHANGED THE IDEA THAT
SNOWBOARDING WAS A MEN'S-ONLY SPORT.

. . .

SHE IS A WORLD SUPERPIPE CHAMPION
AND A FIVE-TIME
X GAMES MEDALIST.

. . .

HER LOVE OF THE OUTDOORS
BEGAN IN THE SIXTH GRADE,
WHEN SHE AND HER CLASSMATES CLIMBED A
FOURTEEN-THOUSAND-FOOT MOUNTAIN.

. . .

WHEN GRETCHEN WAS A KID,
SNOWBOARDING WASN'T EVEN ALLOWED
AT MOST MOUNTAIN RESORTS.

When Gretchen Bleiler was ten, her family moved to Aspen, Colorado. She loved the outdoors, building igloos, and skiing with friends. One day, she took a snowboarding lesson. She had so much fun, she began practicing and teaching herself new tricks. By the time she was fifteen, she was so good, the Aspen Valley Snowboard team invited her to compete.

Gretchen had dreams of becoming an Olympic athlete. But there was one problem: snowboarding wasn't an Olympic sport. That all changed in 1998, when Gretchen was seventeen. As soon as she found out the news, she had to try out. She trained hard, and in 2002, she became the first woman in history to land the death-defying Crippler 540—an inverted aerial move with one and a half spins and a back flip. That same year, she tried out for the Olympic team but didn't make it. In 2003, she won a gold medal at the X Games. Three years later, she tried out for the Olympics again. This time she qualified! She took home a silver medal in the halfpipe competition.

When President George W. Bush congratulated the US Olympic team, he said, "You will always be Olympians. The question is: What are you going to do with it?" That's when Gretchen knew she would use her success to bring awareness to climate change issues. She began sharing her experiences of traveling around the world and witnessing the effects of global warming, such as reduced snowpack, shorter winters, and warmer temperatures. Not only do these climate conditions affect snowboarders, they also affect the communities that live in and near the mountains.

Today, Gretchen works with climate change organizations such as Protect Our Winters, which brings together outdoor sports enthusiasts to find ways to slow climate change. She has also asked leaders in Congress to take positive action on the environment. She's doing her part to change the environment in other ways, too. She helps run a reusable water bottle company called ALEX, which stands for Always Live EXtraordinarily. That is just what Gretchen is doing: she's living an extraordinary life, as both a champion snowboarder and an advocate for the environment.

HANNAH COCKROFT

ELITE WHEELCHAIR RACER, BORN 1992

AMAGING FACTS AND UNBELIEVABLE STATS

ONE OF THE SPORTS
HANNAH PLAYED IN SCHOOL
WAS SEATED DISCUS.
...

BEFORE HANNAH RACES,
SHE PAINTS HER NAILS TO MATCH
HER KIT OR HER CHAIR.
SHE ALSO HAS LUCKY UNDERWEAR
AND LUCKY SOCKS.
...

HER BIGGEST CAREER INFLUENCES:
HER PARENTS,
GRAHAM AND RACHEL.
...

T34 IS A SPORT CLASSIFICATION
FOR PEOPLE WITH CERTAIN
DISABILITIES LIKE HANNAH'S.

Hannah Cockroft loves a challenge. This gold medal Paralympian and ten-time world champion grew up in the United Kingdom with one dream: she wanted to be famous.

Two days after she was born, Hannah suffered an injury that damaged her brain and deformed her legs. Doctors told her parents that Hannah would never walk. She defied the odds and, at age three, took her first steps. This fighting spirit has guided Hannah throughout her life, proving that nothing will hold her back.

As a young child, Hannah wanted to be a ballerina even though she had difficulty walking. She joined a creative dance class and began taking lessons. At thirteen, a wheelchair basketball coach asked her to join the team. Soon after that, she took up wheelchair racing. Next, Hannah joined the Great Britain Paralympic Development Team, achieving elite status within just three years.

In 2010, Hannah broke her first world record in the 400-meter T34 race. In June of that year, she broke seven world records in eight days, all while completing her school exams and being crowned Prom Queen. The following year, she won two gold medals during the IPC Athletics World Championships. That's when she earned her nickname Hurricane Hannah. At the 2012 London Paralympics, Hurricane Hannah was the first Paralympian to break a world record when she won the 100-meter T34. Four years later, at the Rio Paralympics, she took home three gold medals. She now holds the Paralympic record for the T34 100-, 200-, 400-, and 800-meter races.

Hannah is a disability advocate. She speaks out about how it can be difficult for people with disabilities to shop or find homes that accommodate their needs.

She is also an ambassador for many organizations that support people with disabilities, including The 53 Foundation and Forget Me Not Children's Hospice. She actively promotes the benefits of disability sport and encourages people to both watch and support it.

Not only has Hannah achieved her dreams of fame, she is using that fame to help others live their best life.

MISTY COPELAND

BOUNDARY–BREAKING BALLERINA, BORN 1982

AMAZING FACTS AND UNBELIEVABLE STATS

IN 2009, MISTY WENT ON
A YEARLONG TOUR
WITH THE MEGA–FAMOUS
MUSICIAN PRINCE
AND APPEARED IN ONE OF HIS MUSIC VIDEOS.

...

SHE WROTE A
CHILDREN'S BOOK
TITLED *FIREBIRD*.

...

MISTY PLAYED
THE ROLE OF CLARA
IN *THE NUTCRACKER*
FOR THE AMERICAN BALLET THEATRE.

At thirteen, Misty Copeland took her first ballet lesson on a basketball court at the Boys & Girls Club community center in her hometown of San Pedro, California. In the ballet world, thirteen is considered late to start lessons, but Misty caught on quickly and was dancing professionally just a year later. At fifteen, she won first place in the Music Center Spotlight Awards. She enrolled in the San Francisco Ballet School and soon earned a National Training Scholarship from the American Ballet Theatre (ABT)—one of the greatest dance companies in the world. Six years later, she became the second African American soloist ever to perform for the ABT. In 2015, Misty made history once again as the first African American principal female ballet dancer for the ABT!

Ballerinas haven't always been considered athletes, but Misty is changing that. She works and trains as hard as any other athlete, and looks graceful doing it! A typical day for her includes a ninety-minute dance class and seven hours of rehearsals.

Misty faced a lot of criticism on the way to the top. She was told to lose weight, that she didn't have the right body type to be a ballet dancer, and that she was too muscular. She refused to listen and continued her journey to become a boundary-breaking ballerina. But in 2012, Misty's career almost ended when she suffered six stress fractures in her leg and was told she would never dance again. Luckily, she found a doctor who put a metal plate in her leg so she could continue to perform. She was so determined to dance again, she even practiced ballet lying down while she recuperated. A year later, she was back on stage.

Misty is not only an iconic dancer, she is a strong advocate for diversity, especially for women of color. As someone who fell in love with ballet at the Boys & Girls Club, she understands how important it is to have community centers in underprivileged areas. That's why she helped create Project Plié, an initiative that pairs the ABT with Boys & Girls Clubs to mentor young dancers. When she joined Under Armour's motivational campaign "I Will What I Want," she became the first classical dancer to have a sports brand endorsement. She's even written a book called *Ballerina Body* for girls to learn how to care for their bodies as they grow. Misty is a role model for future ballerinas and anyone with big dreams.

DIANE CRUMP

REVOLUTIONARY KENTUCKY DERBY JOCKEY, BORN 1948

AMAZING FACTS AND UNBELIEVABLE STATS

DIANE'S HORSE BRIDLE 'N BIT
FINISHED NINTH OUT OF TWELVE
IN DIANE'S FIRST RACE.

...

IN ONE FAMOUS RACE,
A MALE JOCKEY WAS HOLDING ON TO
DIANE'S HORSE TO SLOW HER DOWN.
SHE TRIED TO FIGHT HIM OFF.
WHEN THE RACE WAS OVER,
THE CROWD THREW
TOMATOES AND EGGS AT HIM.

...

DIANE WAS THE FIRST
OF ONLY SIX WOMEN WHO HAVE EVER
RACED IN THE KENTUCKY DERBY.

Would you believe there was a time when women weren't allowed to race horses? A little more than fifty years ago, only men were allowed to compete. Diane Crump, along with a small group of courageous women, changed all that when they fought for their right to be jockeys.

Diane's love of riding began the first time she rode a pony as a child. As a teen, she worked on a farm grooming and exercising horses. Soon, she was galloping horses at Florida Downs, a horse racing facility. She dreamed of becoming a jockey, but as a girl, she knew she wasn't allowed to race. Then a woman named Kathy Kusner sued the Maryland Racing Commission to get a license to become a jockey. Kathy won her court case but was injured and couldn't race. Diane decided to go for her own license.

In 1969, after winning her license in court, Diane made history. She became the first female jockey to compete in the United States when she raced a horse named Bridle 'n Bit at the Hialeah Park Race Track in Florida. Diane needed a police escort onto the grounds because people were angry. They said she would ruin horse racing. Track officials tried to block her path, and male jockeys refused to compete in races that included women. But Diane ignored them all and continued to race.

In 1970, at the age of twenty-one, she became the first female jockey to compete in the Kentucky Derby, one of the most famous horse races of all time! She raced her horse, Fathom, and came in fifteenth out of seventeen. It didn't matter that she was a long shot. For Diane, it was a dream come true. She went on to win 228 races throughout her career.

After Diane retired, she began a business that helps people buy and sell horses. She also speaks out about how girls should feel confident enough to accomplish their goals and not let anyone or anything stand in their way. Diane's passion for riding and her refusal to take no for an answer paved the way for women to pursue horse racing.

SASHA DIGIULIAN

COMPETITIVE ROCK CLIMBER, BORN 1992

AMASING FACTS AND UNBELIEVABLE STATS

IN 2021, THE US OLYMPICS
ADDED SPORT CLIMBING
FOR BOTH MEN AND WOMEN
FOR THE FIRST TIME EVER.

...

SASHA HAS MADE ADVOCACY
HER LIFE'S WORK.

...

SHE WRITES A COLUMN
FOR *OUTSIDE MAGAZINE*.

...

WHEN SASHA'S NOT CLIMBING,
SHE ENJOYS WRITING, SKIING, SWIMMING,
TRAVELING, AND EXPLORING.

When Sasha DiGiulian was six years old, she attended her brother's birthday party at a climbing gym. She had so much fun, she began climbing twice a week. One day, she signed up for a climbing competition and won. That's when she knew that climbing was more than just a hobby.

When Sasha scaled Pure Imagination in Kentucky, she became the first North American woman in history to complete the grade 9a 5.14d—one of the hardest sport climbs in the world. She has accomplished more than thirty first-female ascents around the globe, including Eiger Mountain, nicknamed Murder Wall. She is also the first woman to free-climb Mora Mora, a twenty-three-hundred-foot ascent. She has won the World Championships for Female Overall, earned silver in the Bouldering World Championships, and won a bronze medal in the Duel. She is also a three-time US national champion and has been the undefeated Pan American Champion since 2004.

As a woman in a sport made up mostly of men, Sasha knows how important it is to create equal opportunities for women. She inspires young girls to follow their passion. That's why she has created and participates in women's climbing workshops.

Sasha is also a global athlete ambassador for Right to Play and Up2Us Sports. These are organizations that encourage children to participate in sports to help them face challenges in both their lives and their communities.

She spends a lot of her time in nature, so she understands how important it is to keep the environment safe. She has teamed up with the American Alpine Club and the Access Fund to find ways to help slow climate change. She even met with representatives in Congress to discuss land conservation.

After a fellow rock climber bullied her online, Sasha began speaking out about cyberbullying and how people need to take responsibility for their actions. She continues to spread her love of climbing while being a shining example for women in adventure and actions sports.

GABBY DOUGLAS

EXTRAORDINARY ARTISTIC GYMNAST, BORN 1995

AMAGING FACTS and UNBELIEVABLE STATS

GABBY'S FAVORITE EVENTS ARE FLOOR EXERCISE AND BEAM.

...

IN 2012, SHE BECAME THE **FIRST AMERICAN TO WIN** BOTH INDIVIDUAL AND TEAM ALL-AROUND GOLD MEDALS AT A SINGLE OLYMPICS.

...

HER FIRST GOLD MEDAL **WAS AT THE 2010** PAN AMERICAN CHAMPIONSHIPS, **WHERE SHE WON** THE UNEVEN BARS TITLE.

Do you have a nickname? Gabby Douglas does! This three-time Olympic gold medalist is called the Flying Squirrel because of her ability to gain extraordinary height during her routine. This incredible feat comes as no surprise. When she was a toddler, she taught herself to do a one-armed cartwheel, flying off the furniture at home. By the time she was nine, Gabby knew that one day she'd become an Olympic gold medalist.

At fourteen, Gabby left her home in Virginia Beach to live with a host family in Iowa, where she could train with a top coach. She missed her family, but she knew she would have to work hard and continue to make sacrifices to reach the top. It wasn't easy.

In 2011, Gabby performed in the National Championships and fell seven times! She was embarrassed, but her mother said, "That's what a winner is—when you fall and you get right back up, and you don't quit." Later that year, she helped her team win the gold at the World Championships. A year later, Gabby's dream came true when she competed in the London Summer Olympics, becoming the first woman of color and the first African American to win the gold medal for Individual All-Around Champion. After that, she collected medals at the World Championships and the AT&T American Cup.

In 2016, Gabby and her team, known as The Final Five, competed in the Rio Olympics. Only this time, Gabby was bullied on the internet. People made fun of her facial expressions and her hair, and because she didn't put her hand on her heart during the national anthem. She was hurt, but she ignored the haters, and her team won the gold. When the Games were over, Gabby began sharing her experience, taking a stand against cyberbullying.

A year later, Mattel released the Gabby Douglas Barbie doll as part of its Shero collection. One of Gabby's many goals is to inspire African American girls to compete in gymnastics. She teamed up with Nike to participate in an equality campaign to remind people that hard work and determination can get you anywhere you want to be.

GRETE ELIASSEN

DARING FREESKIER, BORN 1986

AMESTAMP AMAZING FACTS AND UNBELIEVABLE STATS

WHEN GRETE ISN'T ON THE SNOW,
SHE'S ON THE WATER.
SHE LOVES TO WATER SKI,
STEREO SKI, AND IS A BIG
FAN OF WAKEBOARDING.

...

SHE MADE A MOVIE
CALLED *SAY MY NAME*,
ABOUT ALL-GIRL FREESTYLE SKIING.

...

WHEN SHE WAS TRAINING,
PART OF HER ROUTINE WAS TO DO
300 SIT-UPS A DAY.

When Grete Eliassen began freeskiing, women weren't allowed to compete in major competitions. But that wasn't going to stop her from earning a place on the slopes.

Grete's passion for skiing began when she was just two years old, living in the mountains of Minnesota. As she got older, she participated in hockey, soccer, basketball, tennis, and cross-country and alpine skiing. At the age of ten, she discovered slalom ski racing. A *slalom* is a ski race down a winding course between obstacles such as flags and poles.

When Grete was thirteen, her family moved to Norway, where she continued to tear up the snow. A year later, she won the Norwegian slalom National Championships and joined the Norwegian ski team. Then she won third place in slalom at the European Junior Olympics. At sixteen, Grete began focusing her efforts on freeskiing—an action-packed sport involving speed, jumps, and complicated midair tricks. In 2004, she won the US Freeskiing Open for the first time. The year after that, she became the first female skier to win the Winter X Games.

Grete continued shredding mountains and collecting wins. In 2010, reaching speeds of sixty miles per hour, she won the world record for the Hip Jump. She soared a whopping thirty-one feet in the air! No other woman in history has even come close to that height. She has won the US Freeskiing Open four times and has taken six medals at the Winter X Games, including two golds. She is also the only skier to win medals in the first halfpipe and the slopestyle events. In 2012, after recovering from a knee injury, Grete strapped on her skis and won a bronze at the Norwegian World Championships.

When Grete won the gold in the X Games, her prize money was $2,000. The male prize winner won $45,000! That's why she has made it her mission to knock down gender barriers. In 2017, she was elected president of the Women's Sports Foundation, an organization that helps provide girls equal access in sports. Today she continues her fight for all athletes to have safe, equal rights regardless of gender, race, ethnicity, or ability.

MARLEN ESPARZA

POWERFUL FLYWEIGHT BOXER, BORN 1989

AMANG FACTS & UNBELIEVABLE STATS

AS A CHILD, MARLEN WAS TOLD TO CHOOSE
BETWEEN BOXING AND DANCE.
SHE CHOSE BOXING.

...

SHE IS THE 2006
WORLD CHAMPIONSHIP
BRONZE MEDALIST.

...

WOMEN'S BOXING
MADE ITS DEBUT AT THE
2012 LONDON OLYMPICS.

...

BESIDES BOXING, MARLEN ALSO
LOVES RUNNING.

When Marlen Esparza first became interested in boxing, the coach at the gym didn't want to train her because she was a girl. She would not give up and kept insisting.

Marlen wasn't always the best student and was even considered a trouble-maker. So, her father made a deal with her: if she wanted to box, she'd need to get good grades. She agreed to her father's deal, and they convinced the coach to train her. She began her training at eleven years old, and by sixteen she was the youngest woman to win the National Boxing Championship.

Boxing gave Marlen the focus and confidence she needed. By senior year of high school, she was earning straight A's and was the class president. But then, she had a tough choice to make. Instead of college, she chose to pursue a full-time boxing career. In 2012, Marlen became the first-ever American female boxer to qualify for the Olympics, where she competed and took home a bronze medal.

Two years later, Marlen took the gold at the Women's World Boxing Championships. She was ranked as the number one US flyweight boxer for ten years in a row and is a nine-time US national champion.

Marlen eventually turned pro, becoming the first woman to sign with Golden Boy Boxing, a promotional company. When she became pregnant, she continued training the entire time. Three months after giving birth to a baby boy, she was back in the ring for a fight and won all eight rounds, becoming the North American Boxing Organization Flyweight Champion.

Marlen had to prove herself, and people didn't always take her seriously because she was a girl. Some people even made fun of her. As the first Latina boxer, she speaks to Latinx communities about empowerment and dreaming big. But Marlen is known for more than just her powerful punches. She has paired up with PETA (People for the Ethical Treatment of Animals) to help prevent animal cruelty.

Marlen knows that the path to success isn't easy, but that hasn't stopped her, and she hopes it won't stop anybody else.

LISA FERNANDEZ

RECORD–SETTING SOFTBALL PITCHER AND COACH, BORN 1971

AMAGING FACTS AND UNBELIEVABLE STATS

LISA IS A THREE-TIME
PAN AMERICAN GOLD MEDALIST
AND A FOUR-TIME WORLD CHAMPION.

...

HER FATHER WAS A SEMI-PRO BASEBALL PLAYER IN CUBA.
HER MOTHER, WHO EMIGRATED FROM PUERTO RICO AS A TEEN, USED TO
PLAY SLOW-PITCH SOFTBALL.

...

SHE SET AN OLYMPIC RECORD
FOR THE HIGHEST BATTING AVERAGE—.545.

...

SHE PLAYED BOTH BASKETBALL
AND SOFTBALL IN COLLEGE
AND ALSO LOVES GOLF.

On rainy days, growing up in California, Lisa Fernandez would turn her living room into a stadium and ask her parents to throw balled-up socks to her so she could dive for them. When she began playing softball competitively at the age of eight, she pitched so poorly she walked twenty players and her team lost 28–0. She vowed to do better the next time.

At thirteen, Lisa's softball coach told her she'd never make it as a professional athlete because her arms were too short. Instead of giving up, Lisa took that as a challenge. She practiced so much, her parents hired a private trainer. It wasn't long before she proved her softball coach wrong. Soon her pitches clocked in at a whopping sixty-eight miles per hour, and she became known for her "windmill" style, where her arms whip around.

In high school, Lisa had seventy shutouts in a row. That's when a pitcher pitches a whole game without allowing the opposing team to score. In college, she helped her school win two NCAA Women's College World Series Championships. In 1996, 2000, and 2004, Lisa competed in the Olympics, winning gold each time and striking out twenty-five batters in a single Olympic game. During her Olympic career, she set a record of fifty-nine strikeouts.

The US Olympic Committee named Lisa a Top 10 Athlete of the Year. She's also a two-time Amateur Softball Association (ASA) Sportswoman of the Year, a nine-time ASA All-American, and a six-time MVP. In other words, Lisa is a record-breaking athlete! In 2013, this superstar was inducted into the ASA/USA Softball Hall of Fame.

Lisa represents her Hispanic culture with pride and inspires young Latina athletes to play hard. The Phoenix Mercury, a professional women's basketball team, named her a Woman of Inspiration for her dedication to her work, her community, and her family. She is widely considered one of the ten most influential Hispanic women in sports. Lisa has made it her mission to mentor girls and encourage their passion for the game by coaching the UCLA softball team. Her advice to young people: "You create your own destiny."

ALTHEA GIBSON

TRAILBLAZING TENNIS PLAYER, BORN 1927–DIED 2003

AMAGING FACTS & UNBELIEVABLE STATS

IN 1980, ALTHEA WAS INDUCTED INTO
THE INTERNATIONAL WOMEN'S SPORTS HALL OF FAME.

...

TWO NEW YORK CITY TICKER TAPE PARADES
WERE THROWN IN HER HONOR.

...

SHE PLAYED FOR THE
HARLEM GLOBETROTTERS.

...

IN 1958, THE ASSOCIATED PRESS
VOTED HER FEMALE ATHLETE OF THE YEAR.

Growing up in Harlem, a New York City neighborhood, Althea Gibson hated school, but she loved sports, especially Ping-Pong. At fourteen, she began playing tennis, and a year later she won her first tournament. Soon Althea had enough wins to qualify for the US Nationals. Unfortunately, the organization wouldn't let her play because of her skin color. Another tennis player, Alice Marble, wrote an article about the discrimination Althea faced in a magazine called *American Lawn Tennis*. After the article came out, event organizers changed their mind and invited Althea to participate. At twenty-three, Althea became the first African American player allowed to compete in the US Nationals.

Though Althea had accomplished so much, she continued to face a lot of discrimination. People refused her membership to their clubs. When she was traveling, hotels wouldn't give her a room. One refused to hold a lunch in her honor. So much of the sport was closed to Althea, but this slowly began to change. In 1951, she became the first African American invited to play at Wimbledon. Two years later, Althea was one of the top ten players in the United States.

It wasn't long before Althea made history again. She was the first African American to win the French Championships. She was also the first African American to win both Wimbledon and the US Nationals. Then she became the first African American woman to appear on the covers of *Time* magazine and *Sports Illustrated*.

In 1959, as the number one ranked tennis player in the world, Althea turned pro. Then she began playing golf. In another history-making feat, she became the first African American to compete in the Ladies Professional Golf Association Tour. By 1971, she had won eleven Grand Slam events in tennis and was inducted into the International Tennis Hall of Fame.

Althea was an equal rights pioneer, paving the way for other athletes of color. In a now famous quote, she explains, "I always wanted to be somebody. If I made it, it's half because I was game enough to take a lot of punishment along the way and half because there were a lot of people who cared enough to help me."

BETHANY HAMILTON

FEARLESS SURFER, BORN 1990

AMALING FACTS AND UNBELIEVABLE STATS

BETHANY'S SHARK-BITTEN SURFBOARD IS ON DISPLAY AT THE CALIFORNIA SURF MUSEUM.

...

AN INSPIRING MOVIE ABOUT BETHANY'S LIFE CALLED *SOUL SURFERS* WAS RELEASED IN 2011.

...

HER NICKNAME IS B-HAM OR BETHY.

Thirteen-year-old surfing star Bethany Hamilton was floating face-down on her surfboard with one arm dangling in the water when the unthinkable happened: a fourteen-foot tiger shark attacked her just off the coast of Kauai in Hawaii. Luckily, her quick-thinking friend helped her get to shore. Bethany was rushed to the hospital. She survived but lost her arm and 60 percent of her blood. Less than one month after the shark attack, despite her physical challenges, she returned to competitive surfing.

Bethany began surfing at the age of seven. She won her first-ever surfing contest at eight. By nine she had signed her first major sponsorship deal. After the shark attack, Bethany was determined to get right back on her board. It took practice, but she learned to adjust her technique to make up for her missing arm. Two years later, she won her first national surfing title. This showed her dedication and perseverance, making her an icon.

At seventeen, Bethany began surfing professionally. At a World Surf League competition, she beat a six-time world champion and the top-ranked surfer in the world. She also surfed one of the most famous waves in the world known as Jaws. In 2017, this unstoppable wave rider was inducted into the Surfers' Hall of Fame.

Bethany has dedicated her life to helping others. She started a nonprofit organization called Friends of Bethany, which assists people who have lost limbs. She takes young people with limb differences surfing, and helps them finds ways to overcome their fears. She also leads a surf camp through Make-A-Wish Foundation. This is an organization that helps fulfill the wishes of children with critical illnesses.

Bethany is an author and motivational speaker. She talks about why it's important for people to pursue their dreams no matter the obstacles. In 2018, she released a film called *Unstoppable*. It is based on her book *Be Unstoppable: The Art of Never Giving Up*. She wants young girls to be courageous and meet whatever challenges come their way. Bethany has faced her own challenges and is pretty tough. That's why her motto is Surfs Like a Girl.

MIA HAMM

SUPERSTAR SOCCER PLAYER, BORN 1972

AMANDA FACTS <small>AND</small> UNBELIEVABLE STATS

IN 2007, MIA WAS INDUCTED
INTO THE NATIONAL
SOCCER HALL OF FAME.

...

NIKE NAMED THE
LARGEST BUILDING
ON ITS CAMPUS AFTER HER.

...

IN 2012, ESPN NAMED HER
THE GREATEST
FEMALE ATHLETE
OF THE PAST FORTY YEARS.

When Mia Hamm was a young girl, her family moved around a lot because her father was in the Air Force. One way she made friends was by playing soccer. She was really good at it. By the time she was fifteen, Mia had become the youngest player on the US national team. At nineteen, she became the youngest team member in history to win the World Cup. Whenever she played, the opposing team named her "the player to be stopped." She always had two or three defenders trying to block her. But that just made Mia play harder.

In 1996, Mia led the US women's soccer team to Olympic gold. It wasn't long before she was considered the first international female soccer star. Jerseys with the number 9—her number—became best sellers. Three years later, Mia helped her team win another World Cup. She was named the FIFA World Player of the Year—not once but twice, in 2001 and 2002! Two years later, she led her team to Olympic gold once again. That same year, Mia made FIFA's list of 125 greatest living soccer players.

Mia retired in 2004, but not before taking the record for most international goals scored ever: 158. She held that record until 2013, when US player Abby Wambach took the title.

Mia's excitement for the sport opened up soccer to a whole generation of girls. Today she is considered one of the most important people in sports history. She uses her popularity to empower girls and promote gender equality. She even filmed a television commercial with basketball player Michael Jordon called "Anything You Can Do I Can do Better." She wanted to prove to the world that girls could do anything boys could do!

Today, Mia continues to give back by running the Mia Hamm Foundation, which helps develop programs for girls to compete in sports. It also raises awareness about cord blood and bone marrow transplants, helping to support patients and their families. Mia now spends much of her time raising her twin girls and encouraging kids to play at the top of their game.

JACKIE JOYNER-KERSEE

WORLD–CLASS TRACK AND FIELDER, BORN 1962

AMAGING FACTS AND UNBELIEVABLE STATS

JACKIE WROTE A BOOK CALLED

A WOMAN'S PLACE IS EVERYWHERE.

...

THE SEVEN HEPTATHLON

EVENTS ARE:

100-METER HURDLES, HIGH JUMP,
SHOT PUT, 200 METERS, LONG JUMP,
JAVELIN THROW, 800 METERS

...

UCLA NAMED JACKIE ONE OF

THE 15 GREATEST BASKETBALL PLAYERS

IN UCLA WOMEN'S BASKETBALL HISTORY.

Jackie Joyner-Kersee was the first woman in history to score over 7,000 points in the heptathlon. A *heptathlon* is a track-and-field competition made up of seven events that take place over two days. Jackie is also a six-time Olympic medalist, holds records in the long jump, and was a world-class 100- and 200-meter runner. Oh, and she also had a successful basketball career!

As a child growing up in a tough East St. Louis, Illinois, neighborhood, Jackie stayed out of trouble by focusing on both her education and sports. After school, she would go to her community center to shoot hoops with other kids. By the time she was in high school, she was playing volleyball, basketball, and running track. At only fourteen years old, Jackie won four junior pentathlon championships for track and field! Her all-around athletic abilities were rewarded. When she applied to college, she won a basketball scholarship.

In 1984, Jackie took time off from basketball to train for the Summer Olympics heptathlon. She lost the gold by just five points, but won the silver. She promised herself that next time, she'd take the gold. Two years later, she set a world record at the Goodwill Games in Moscow, scoring 7,148 points in the heptathlon. At the 1988 Olympics, she broke that record, scoring 7,291 points in the heptathlon, winning gold along the way. Jackie had fulfilled the promise she had made to herself. Her 7.45-meter long jump also won her a gold medal that year. Jackie's record-breaking streak is so impressive, *Sports Illustrated* called her the greatest female athlete of the twentieth century.

Jackie retired from track and field and played for the American Basketball League for a short time. Now she gives back to the communities that supported her when she was growing up. She focuses on racial equality, social reform, women's rights, health issues, and education. She created the Jackie Joyner-Kersee Foundation to help young people and their families in low-income areas improve their quality of life. The foundation raised over $12 million to help build a sports complex for underserved children in East St. Louis. She also helped found Athletes for Hope. This connects other athletes to charitable causes. Jackie is not only one of the world's best athletes, she is leading the way with her advocacy work.

BILLIE JEAN KING

ICONIC TENNIS PLAYER, BORN 1943

AMAGING FACTS & UNBELIEVABLE STATS

BILLIE JEAN FOUGHT FOR TITLE IX—

A LAW THAT SAYS WOMEN'S SPORTS MUST RECEIVE THE SAME FUNDING IN SCHOOLS AS MEN'S SPORTS.

...

SHE WAS THE FIRST WOMAN TO COACH

A CO-ED TEAM IN PROFESSIONAL SPORTS.

...

IN 1972, BILLIE JEAN BECAME THE

FIRST WOMAN EVER

TO BE NAMED SPORTSPERSON OF THE YEAR BY *SPORTS ILLUSTRATED*.

When Billie Jean King was twelve years old, she wasn't allowed to participate in a group photo at a junior tennis tournament. The reason: she was wearing shorts instead of a skirt. That was the first time she faced discrimination for being a girl. But it wasn't the last. Throughout her career during the 1960s and 1970s, Billie Jean was paid much less money than male tennis players, even when she won! To protest this, she and eight other women formed their own tour called the Virginia Slims Circuit.

Billie Jean was the first female athlete to win over $100,000 in prize money in a single year. That sounds like a lot, but the following year, when she won the US Open, she still earned less than the male champion. Billie Jean began demanding change. She formed the Women's Tennis Association and became its first president.

Two years later, in part because of her efforts, the US Open became the first tournament to offer equal prize money to men and women athletes. That same year, a male tennis player named Bobby Riggs said that women tennis players were not as good as male tennis players. Bobby challenged Billie Jean to a match. At first, she said no, but then she changed her mind and accepted the challenge. The media named the match the "Battle of the Sexes."

Over thirty thousand people attended the match, and ninety million people around the world tuned in to watch on TV. Billie Jean knew she needed to beat Bobby to prove once and for all that women were just as good at sports as men. She beat him in straight sets, taking home the prize money! The win was a turning point in sports history. Girls all over the country began enrolling in sports programs because of Billie Jean.

Throughout her career, Billie Jean won thirty-nine Grand Slam titles, including a record twenty championships at Wimbledon. She also continued to fight for women's equality. She founded a women's sports magazine and many foundations that support equal pay for women. One of them, the Billie Jean King Leadership Initiative, focuses on diversity and inclusiveness at work. She is also an advocate for the LGBTQ community. She was the first openly gay coach of the US women's tennis team. In 2009, President Barack Obama honored her trailblazing accomplishments with the Presidential Medal of Freedom.

PHAIDRA KNIGHT

TOP RUGBY PLAYER, BORN 1974

AMANZING FACTS AND UNBELIEVABLE STATS

IN 2010, *RUGBY MAGAZINE* NAMED PHAIDRA
PLAYER OF THE DECADE.

...

SHE WANTED TO TRY A DIFFERENT SPORT,
SO SHE JOINED THE USA BOBSLED DEVELOPMENT TEAM.
SHE NARROWLY MISSED QUALIFYING
FOR THE OLYMPICS.

...

THE ELITE CLUBS NATIONAL
LEAGUE NAMED PHAIDRA
S'HERO OF THE MONTH
FOR HER LEADERSHIP AND
COMMITMENT TO SPORTS.

Phaidra Knight grew up in the small town of Irwinton, Georgia. Doing chores around her family's farm helped her learn the importance of hard work. This discipline paved the way for her to become one of the greatest rugby players in the United States.

As a child, Phaidra loved football. Unfortunately, she wasn't allowed to play because there were no teams for girls. Instead, she played volleyball and basketball. After graduating college, she enrolled in law school. She had plans to join the basketball team, but a friend suggested she try rugby. She had never heard of the sport, but what could be more fun than tackling team-mates? She showed up to practice and immediately jumped in and started playing. She crushed it!

After that first day of training, Phaidra's life changed. She earned her degree, but she no longer wanted to practice law. Instead, she pursued her dreams of playing professional rugby.

Phaidra played with the US women's national rugby team for twelve years and had thirty-five international appearances. She has participated in three World Cups and has twice been named the top player in the world in her position. In 2017, she became the second woman in the United States to be inducted into the Rugby Hall of Fame. That year she also became the head coach of a women's college rugby team in the Bronx.

When she was training for the Women's Rugby World Cup, she was awarded money to help pay for her training and travel. Now, she's paying it forward. She works with the Women's Sports Foundation to increase funding for athletes in need. She also raises awareness about how difficult it is for women athletes to support themselves while training.

As the director and coach of Play Rugby, she teaches kids in underserved communities. She also coaches rugby for young men in prison. This inspired her to create PeaK Unleashed, a nonprofit that develops leadership skills through rugby for at-risk children. With a background in law and a solid career in sports, Phaidra is using her experience to make positive changes. She is a true social justice warrior.

SILKEN LAUMANN

CHAMPION ROWER, BORN 1964

AMANZING FACTS & UNBELIEVABLE STATS

SCULLS IS A TYPE OF ROWING IN WHICH A BOAT IS PROPELLED BY ONE OR MORE ROWERS WHO EACH HAVE TWO OARS.

...

SILKEN MADE HER OLYMPIC DEBUT IN 1984 ROWING IN DOUBLE SCULLS WITH HER SISTER.

...

SHE HAS BEEN INDUCTED INTO THE CANADIAN OLYMPIC HALL OF FAME, CANADA'S SPORTS HALL OF FAME, AND CANADA'S WALK OF FAME.

...

SHE'S BEEN NAMED CANADA'S FEMALE ATHLETE OF THE YEAR TWO TIMES.

Ten weeks before the 1992 Olympics, Silken Laumann, the single sculls world champion, was in a warm-up area getting ready for a rowing race in Germany. Suddenly, another boat rammed into hers. The accident left her with a shattered leg. Her doctors told her she might never compete again.

Silken had been rowing since the age of seventeen. She wasn't about to let this unfortunate accident ruin everything she had worked so hard to achieve. She spent the next month recovering from five separate operations, determined to compete in the upcoming Olympics. Despite her doctor's predictions, she arrived in Barcelona ready to row. She walked up to her boat with the help of a cane. Canadians woke in the middle of the night to watch her race, and she did not disappoint. Silken made the greatest comeback in Canadian sports history, winning the bronze and inspiring an entire nation.

Four years later, she took the silver medal at the Atlanta Olympics. By the time she retired from rowing in 1999, she had three Olympic medals, had taken the single sculls silver medal at the World Championships, and had won the World title.

Silken's accident changed her life. She made it her mission to help people improve their mental and physical health. One of the many ways she did this was to join the Goodlife Kids Foundation, which inspires kids to eat well and stay active. She is also involved with Right to Play. This is an organization that focuses on the importance of play for children in disadvantaged communities around the world. Silken believes that physical activity helps kids focus in school and builds self-esteem.

Silken created a website called We Are Unsinkable. This is a place where people can share their stories about hardship. She knows from experience that the only way to overcome obstacles is through sheer grit and willpower. Now she wants to get the message out and help others achieve their goals.

NANCY LOPEZ

GOLF HALL OF FAMER, BORN 1957

AMAGING FACTS AND UNBELIEVABLE STATS

NANCY WAS ALWAYS KNOWN FOR HER EXCEPTIONAL **KINDNESS TO FANS** WHILE SHE WAS ON TOUR.

...

SHE WAS THE YOUNGEST PERSON EVER TO QUALIFY FOR THE LPGA HALL OF FAME.

...

NANCY KNOWS THE IMPORTANCE OF WINNING, BUT SHE ALSO KNOWS HOW IMPORTANT IT IS TO ACCEPT DEFEAT.

At a time when not many people were interested in golf, Nancy Lopez came on the scene and shook things up. At the age of twenty-one, she won five tournaments in a row, as well as the Ladies Professional Golf Association (LPGA) Championship. That year, she totaled nine tournament wins, was named Rookie of the Year and LPGA Player of the Year, and won the Vare Trophy—awarded to the golfer with the lowest scoring average. She was the only golfer in history to win all three awards in one season! Suddenly, people were paying attention. The following year, she won eight more tournaments!

Nancy began playing golf when she was eight and won her first golf tournament at nine years old. Three years later, she won her first New Mexico Women's Amateur Championship, becoming the youngest winner in the state's history. Nancy was the only girl on her golf team in high school, but that didn't intimidate her. She led them to the state championship! As a senior, she finished second at the US Women's Open. Soon she became known as one of the greatest golfers of all time.

At thirty-five, Nancy had so many wins, she was inducted into the LPGA Hall of Fame. Her record-setting stroke average was 70.73. When she retired, she had forty-eight LPGA victories and had been named Player of the Year four times!

Before Nancy became famous, golf was considered a sport for rich men. This meant that a lot of people who wanted to play couldn't afford it. Nancy is helping to change that by providing opportunities for young golfers. She has joined up with many charities, including Adventures in Movement, an organization that supports people with disabilities.

In 2013, ESPN voted her the most influential Hispanic athlete of all time. She continues to give back by helping make golf accessible to Hispanic children. She also encourages women to play by mentoring young female golfers, and she heads an organization called Nancy Lopez Adventures. Nancy inspires others to believe in themselves and never doubt their own abilities.

TATYANA MCFADDEN

CELEBRATED WHEELCHAIR RACER
AND NORDIC SKIER, BORN 1989

AMAZING FACTS AND UNBELIEVABLE STATS

. . . .

TATYANA LOVES
SCUBA DIVING, JET SKIING, AND PARASAILING.

. . .

TATYANA'S WHEELCHAIR DOESN'T HAVE GEARS.
IT IS POWERED BY THE STRENGTH OF HER ARMS.
SHE TRAINS 2 TO 4 HOURS A DAY AND LOGS OVER 100 MILES A WEEK.

. . .

SHE WON THE BOSTON MARATHON FOR THE WOMEN'S WHEELCHAIR DIVISION IN 2018 AND CAME IN SECOND IN 2019.

Tatyana McFadden was born with a condition called spina bifida and is paralyzed from the waist down. She spent the first years of her life in an orphanage in Russia. She didn't have a wheelchair, so she learned to walk on her hands. It was the only way she could keep up with other children. At six years old, she was adopted and moved to the United States. That was when she began using a wheelchair for the first time. To stay strong, she enrolled in wheelchair basketball, track and field, swimming, and other sports.

It wasn't long before Tatyana chose to focus on wheelchair racing. But in high school, she was told that she wasn't allowed to compete because her wheelchair was a hazard to others. She and her mother sued the Howard County Public School system, and Tatyana won the right to race with her classmates. Winning this lawsuit was important not only for Tatyana but for other athletes with disabilities. It paved the way for the passage of a law that requires schools to allow students with disabilities to compete in interscholastic sports.

When Tatyana was fifteen, she became the youngest athlete on the US Paralympic Track and Field team. She won both a silver and a bronze medal in the 2004 Paralympic Games. Two years later, she won the gold at the World Championships and set a new record in the 100-meter T54 event. Her athletic skills continued to pay off. At the 2008 Paralympics, she took home four medals. In 2012, she won four more, and in 2013, she won six gold medals in the World Championships! Then, she became the first person ever to win four major marathons in one year.

In 2014, Tatyana became a two-sport Paralympian. She competed in Nordic skiing at the Paralympic Games in Russia, where she won silver. At the 2016 Paralympics, she dominated in wheelchair racing, winning four golds and two silvers. That year, she held the world records in the T54 100-, 400-, 800-, 1,500-, and 5,000-meter races.

When Tatyana is not on the track, she's advocating for equal opportunities for people with disabilities. She is an ambassador for the New York Roadrunner Team for Kids, where she has helped start a wheelchair racing program. She was given the Wilma Rudolph Courage Award for overcoming adversity while serving as a role model to others.

IBTIHAJ MUHAMMAD

BARRIER–BREAKING SABER FENCER, BORN 1985

AMANG FACTS AND UNBELIEVABLE STATS

IBTIHAJ HAS HER OWN CLOTHING LINE **CALLED LOUELLA,** WHICH SELLS MODEST FASHIONABLE CLOTHING.

...

HER TEAM TOOK HOME THE GOLD AT THE PAN AMERICAN GAMES IN 2011 AND 2015.

...

SHE IS A SPORTS AMBASSADOR FOR THE **EMPOWERING WOMEN AND GIRLS THROUGH SPORTS INITIATIVE.** SHE ALSO WORKS WITH ATHLETES FOR IMPACT AND THE SPECIAL OLYMPICS.

Growing up in New Jersey was challenging for Ibtihaj Muhammad. People had a difficult time pronouncing her name. They stared at her because she dressed modestly and was very religious. But like other children, Ibtihaj rode her bike, went camping, and took family vacations.

When Ibtihaj was twelve, her parents encouraged her to play sports. Fencing was the perfect choice because the uniform covered her entire body, a religious requirement for her. But Ibtihaj also liked fencing because it was fast and competitive.

Ibtihaj's high school team made the state championships, and she went on to the Junior Olympics. She was so good, she earned a scholarship to Duke University. Once there, life was difficult. Teammates made racist jokes and were unkind to her because of the way she dressed and because of the color of her skin. Sadly, she chose to give up fencing.

When she returned home, her former high school coach encouraged her to start fencing again with the goal of making the Olympic team. By 2013, Ibtihaj had become a top ten world-ranking and US champion. By 2015, she had won five World Championships!

The following year, Ibtihaj's dreams came true when she made the US Women's Saber Fencing Team. But she faced discrimination again. Her teammates ignored her, and even her Olympic coach wasn't nice. Nevertheless, she kept her focus and won the bronze. Ibtihaj was the first US Olympian ever to compete in a hijab. When the Olympics were over, she became the first Muslim American to stand on the podium with her medal.

Now Ibtihaj is an activist, a speaker, and an entrepreneur who models tolerance and kindness. She speaks about diversity, inclusion, leadership, and overcoming obstacles. She has even written a children's book called *The Proudest Blue* about finding ways to be strong. In 2017, Mattel launched its first Barbie with a hijab in her honor as part of their Shero collection. Ibtihaj has been named one of *Time* magazine's 100 Most Influential People. This is in part because of her mission to bring awareness to the issue of equality around the world, especially when it comes to sports.

DANICA PATRICK

PROFESSIONAL RACE CAR DRIVER, BORN 1982

AMGAZING FACTS AND UNBELIEVABLE STATS

IN 2005, SHE WAS NAMED
ROOKIE OF THE YEAR.

...

DANICA WAS VOTED
INDY RACING LEAGUE MOST POPULAR DRIVER
THREE YEARS IN A ROW.

...

SHE IS A THREE-TIME WINNER
OF THE WORLD KARTING ASSOCIATION
GRAND NATIONAL CHAMPIONSHIPS.

...

DANICA WORKS WITH MAKE-A-WISH FOUNDATION
TO HELP CHILDREN WITH TERMINAL
ILLNESSES FULFILL THEIR DREAMS.

anica Patrick's need for speed began when she took up go-kart racing at age ten. She loved it so much that at sixteen, she left school and headed to Great Britain to pursue auto racing. She won second place in the super competitive Formula Ford Festival 2000. It was the best finish ever for an American. But for Danica, it was only the beginning of her history-making career.

In 2004, Danica qualified for the Indianapolis 500, one of the most famous races in the world. Only three other women had ever competed in this race. She led the race for nineteen laps and finished in fourth place. Four years later, she won the Firestone Indy 300 in Japan by 5.86 seconds. This made her the first woman ever to win an IndyCar race.

In her next big career move, she began racing stock cars in NASCAR races. People criticized her, saying race car driving was a men's sport. That wasn't about to stop Danica from doing what she enjoyed most. By 2012, this auto racing legend continued to prove just how incredible she was. She started competing in NASCAR's top-tier races. A year later, she became the first woman to win the pole position at the Daytona 500. The pole position is the inside front row starting position, and it's usually given to the driver with the best qualifying time. Danica also holds the title for the best finish by a woman in NASCAR history. In 2013, she raced all thirty-six events in the Sprint Cup Series, a first for a female race car driver.

Danica is on a mission to motivate others. She meets with kids at schools and organizations like the Boys & Girls Club and has helped NASCAR launch its Hall of Fame Kids Club. She is also getting girls interested in STEM— science, technology, engineering, and math. After all, race car drivers depend on engineers and scientists to make sure their cars are safe.

Danica has a podcast called *Pretty Intense*. On the show, she talks about how people can create the life they want for themselves. As the most successful woman in racing history, her message is: "Work hard and appreciate your own self-worth."

MEGAN RAPINOE

DOMINATING WORLD CUP SOCCER STAR, BORN 1985

AMAZING FACTS AND UNBELIEVABLE STATS

MEGAN WAS FEATURED IN
FIFA16, A VIDEO GAME SERIES.

...

SEPTEMBER 10 IS MEGAN RAPINOE DAY
IN HER HOMETOWN OF REDDING, CALIFORNIA.

...

AFTER THE 2015 WORLD CUP,
A FARM IN CALIFORNIA MADE A CORN
MAZE IN THE SHAPE OF MEGAN'S FACE.

...

HER CLUB TEAM IS REIGN FC
IN TACOMA, WASHINGTON.

...

SHE IS THE FIRST WOMAN
TO START IN THREE WORLD CUP
FINALS IN A ROW.

It was the 2019 World Cup Final. The United States was playing the Netherlands in a sold-out stadium filled with 57,900 fans. At halftime, the score was 0-0. The players were feeling the pressure. At the sixty-one-minute mark, Megan Rapinoe scored on a penalty kick. The final tally was 2-0 Team USA. That day, Megan became the first woman ever to score on a penalty kick in the final. It was also the first time in history a winning team held four World Cup titles.

Megan scored six goals during the tournament, three on penalty kicks. She won the Golden Ball for best player and the Golden Boot for leading scorer of the tournament, and she was named Player of the Match. But this came as no surprise to her teammates.

In the 2011 World Cup quarterfinals, she sent a fifty-yard cross to Abby Wambach in overtime, helping win the game. After that match, ESPN named her Next Level Player of the Week. The following year, she scored three goals in the 2012 London Olympics. She is the only player, man or woman, to ever score directly from a corner kick at an Olympic game.

In 2015, Megan once again helped lead Team USA to World Cup victory. That was the first time a US women's sports team was honored with a ticker tape parade in New York City.

In 2019, as the FIFA president handed out the medals to Team USA, the crowd chanted, "Equal pay, equal pay." That's because the previous year, the prize money for the men's soccer team was $400 million. The women were only getting paid $30 million for their win. Megan is fighting to close this wage gap. She and her teammates sued the United States Soccer Federation for gender discrimination. Now they are demanding equal pay. That same year, *Sports Illustrated* named Megan Sportsperson of the Year for being an agent of change, both on the field and out in the world.

As a gay woman, Megan is an advocate for LGBTQ equality in sports. She works with the Gay, Lesbian & Straight Education Network and Athlete Ally to make sure everyone has the chance to play.

She and her twin sister, Rachel, also run a soccer club called Rapinoe SC. They teach kids to work hard, have fun, and dream big. Megan helps empower young people to make a difference not only in their communities but in the world. Her motto is Be Your Best You.

MARY LOU RETTON

GOLD MEDAL OLYMPIC GYMNAST, BORN 1968

AMAGING FACTS & UNBELIEVABLE STATS

IN 1984, *SPORTS ILLUSTRATED*
NAMED MARY LOU
SPORTSWOMAN OF THE YEAR.

...

IN 1994, THE US OLYMPICS COMMITTEE
BEGAN HONORING ATHLETES WITH
THE MARY LOU RETTON AWARD
FOR ATHLETIC EXCELLENCE.

...

MARY LOU HAD KNEE SURGERY
FIVE WEEKS BEFORE THE 1984 OLYMPICS.

When Mary Lou Retton was eight years old, she watched Romanian gymnast Nadia Comaneci score seven perfect 10s at the US Olympics. That was the moment Mary Lou knew that she wanted to stand on the Olympic podium just like Nadia.

Mary Lou began entering gymnastics competitions. One day at a competition in Nevada, the famous gymnastics coach Béla Károlyi noticed Mary Lou's talent. Béla offered to coach Mary Lou. At fourteen, she packed her bags and moved to Texas to begin her Olympic training.

Mary Lou didn't practice the fluttery dance moves the sport was known for. Instead, she focused on becoming fast and powerful. Soon, she was racking up wins. She won the American Cup, became the only American to win Japan's Chunichi Cup, and won the USA Gymnastics Federation American Classic twice.

When she qualified for the 1984 Olympics, the pressure was on. In the final events, Romanian gymnast Ecaterina Szabo had just scored 9.9 on the uneven bars. If Mary Lou was going to take the gold, she would have to get a perfect 10. The crowd cheered her on. She nailed both the floor exercise and the vault in a dramatic victory. Sixteen-year-old Mary Lou had just become the first US gymnast in Olympic history to win the All-Around gold medal, scoring not one but two perfect 10s! By the end of the competition, she had won a total of five medals, including two silver and two bronze, more than any other athlete that year.

Mary Lou became known as America's Sweetheart and held the honor of being the first female athlete to appear on the front of the Wheaties cereal box. She was also the first gymnast inducted into the US Olympic Hall of Fame. Her success changed gymnastics for young girls. Now an icon, she has become a fitness ambassador, speaking to communities about nutrition and exercise. She is also a motivational speaker who helps people get out of their comfort zones and go for the gold!

MANON RHÉAUME

HISTORY-MAKING ICE HOCKEY GOALIE, BORN 1972

AMAZING FACTS AND UNBELIEVABLE STATS

MANON BRIEFLY QUIT
PLAYING HOCKEY AT THE
AGE OF SEVENTEEN BECAUSE
OF ALL THE OBSTACLES SHE
FACED AS A GIRL.

...

SHE IS KNOWN AS
THE FIRST WOMAN OF HOCKEY.

...

SHE WON THE GOLD
AT THE 1992 AND 1994 WORLD
HOCKEY CHAMPIONSHIPS.

Manon Rhéaume is used to firsts. She was the first girl to play on a boys' team for the Quebec Pee-Wee International Hockey tournament. She was the first female to play in the Quebec Major Junior Hockey League. And she became the first woman in history to play in a men's major professional sports league when she signed with the Tampa Bay Lightning as a goalie in the National Hockey League (NHL).

Born and raised in Quebec, Canada, Manon's passion for hockey developed at an early age. Unfortunately, there were few opportunities for girls to play at a competitive level. She began trying out for boys' teams, but many officials and parents didn't want her to play. She faced a lot of rejection, but she never gave up. She wanted to play on a professional men's hockey team.

When Manon was twenty, the general manager of the Tampa Bay Lightning was so impressed with her skills, he invited her to the team's training camp. Some said that this was just a publicity stunt, but Manon didn't care what people thought. She was always told she couldn't play because she was a girl. Now, if someone was hiring her *just* because she was a girl, that was fine with her. She knew that no matter what, once she was on the ice, she would have to prove herself and play hard.

In her very first game, she let in only two goals out of nine shots and played for one period. After that historic day, Manon began playing for the Atlanta Knights, a minor league team. From 1992 to 1997, she played twenty-four games over five seasons on men's professional minor league hockey teams. In 1998, the Olympics finally added women's hockey. Manon played for the Canadian team, taking home the silver.

Manon put her love of the sport to good use and began working for Mission Hockey to create hockey products for women. She also created the Manon Rhéaume Foundation to provide scholarships to young female athletes. As of 2021, Manon remains the only woman to have played in an NHL game. Her fearlessness has inspired countless girls to pick up a hockey stick and start playing.

RONDA ROUSEY

STANDOUT MIXED MARTIAL ARTIST, BORN 1987

AMAZING FACTS AND UNBELIEVABLE STATS

RONDA WON THE GOLD
AT THE 2007 PAN AMERICAN GAMES.

...

SHE WON THE BEST FEMALE
ATHLETE ESPY AWARD TWICE.

...

IN JULY 2018, SHE BECAME
THE FIRST WOMAN
TO BE INDUCTED INTO THE
UFC HALL OF FAME.

...

RONDA WAS BORN WITH HER
UMBILICAL CORD AROUND HER NECK,
CUTTING OFF OXYGEN.
AS A KID SHE STRUGGLED TO SPEAK,
BUT SPEECH THERAPY HELPED.

t's no surprise that Ronda Rousey likes to fight. Her mother, AnnMaria De Mars, was an American Judo champion who began training Ronda at the age of eight. At seventeen, Ronda made her debut on the US Olympic judo team. Four years later, she competed in the Olympics again, becoming the first American to win the women's middleweight judo event.

Then, Ronda fell on hard times and took odd jobs to survive. Sometimes she had to sleep in her car. One day, she was watching television and saw a mixed martial arts (MMA) event. That's when she joined Strikeforce, an amateur MMA women's division. She quickly rose to the top.

Now known as Rowdy Ronda, this mixed martial artist was about to forever change the sport. She wanted to fight in the Ultimate Fighting Championship (UFC), but women were not allowed to compete. She put pressure on the organization to create a women's division, won her first fight, and earned her place as the UFC's very first female Bantamweight Champion. Ronda went on to set the record for the most UFC title wins by a woman—six. This powerhouse became known for taking down opponents with her signature armbar move. Most of her fights ended in the first round. The quickest of her twelve MMA wins was only fourteen seconds!

Ronda remained undefeated for four years. In 2015, she was set to fight Holly Holm. It was one of the UFC's best-selling events. Holly was fierce. Ronda used her famous armbar move, but Holly broke free. In a huge upset, Holly took down Ronda with a leg kick and won the match. In 2018, Ronda joined World Wrestling Entertainment as a full-time wrestler and won the Raw Women's Championship. She then competed in the first-ever women's main event at WrestleMania.

Ronda advocates for body positivity and speaks out about mental illness. She had bulimia, an eating disorder, and struggled with her body image. Luckily, with the right support and a lot of determination, she was able to overcome the disorder. Now she embraces the way she looks. Ronda continues to show the world what it really means to fight like a girl.

WILMA RUDOLPH

PIONEERING TRACK AND FIELD STAR, BORN 1940–DIED 1994

AMAMZING FACTS AND UNBELIEVABLE STATS

WILMA'S HIGH SCHOOL BASKETBALL COACH
NICKNAMED HER SKEETER.

...

SHE WON GOLD
AT THE 1959 PAN AMERICAN GAMES.

...

HER THREE GOLDS
AT THE 1960S OLYMPICS
WERE FOR THE 100-METER, 200-METER, AND 4X100-METER RELAY.

...

HER TRACK TEAM AT
TENNESSEE STATE UNIVERSITY WAS
CALLED THE TIGERBELLES.

When Wilma Rudolph was four years old, she was told she would never walk again. She had been diagnosed with a disease called polio. This damaged the nerves in her body. No one could have predicted that one day, she would become known as the fastest woman in the world.

Wilma grew up in Tennessee, one of twenty-two children, and had to wear braces on her legs. Her parents and siblings took care of her. Her mother told her that despite what the doctor had said, one day she would walk again. At age six, with a lot of treatment, Wilma was able to hop on one leg. At eleven, she was playing basketball. In high school, Wilma was so athletic she began competing in track and field on a college level. At sixteen, she became the youngest member to make the 1956 Olympic team. She won a bronze medal in the 400-meter relay. Four years later, she was back at the Olympics. This time, she won three gold medals and broke three world records in track and field. Wilma holds the honor of being the first American in history to take home three golds from a single Olympic Games. Soon after, girls around the globe were inspired to take up the sport because of Wilma.

Even as a heroine, Wilma faced racism. The press reported her wins using racist terms and stereotypes. When her hometown set up a parade in her honor, she refused to attend because it was segregated. With her insistence, local officials finally agreed that everyone could celebrate together. It became the first integrated event in her town.

When she retired at the age of twenty-two, Wilma became a school teacher. She spent the rest of her life protesting and fighting to end segregation laws. She also founded the Wilma Rudolph Foundation, which helped support underserved athletes throughout the United States. Wilma died of cancer at the age of fifty-four. This trailblazing athlete will always be known for defying the odds, fighting racism, and inspiring others to stand up for what's right.

JUNKO TABEI

ADVENTUROUS MOUNTAIN CLIMBER, BORN 1939–DIED 2016

AMAZING FACTS & UNBELIEVABLE STATS

THE SEVEN HIGHEST
SUMMITS IN THE WORLD ARE:
DENALI, KILIMANJARO, MOUNT ACONCAGUA, MOUNT ELBRUS, MOUNT EVEREST, VINSON MASSIF, AND JAYA PEAK.

. . .

JUNKO WAS THE THIRTY–SIXTH PERSON
EVER TO SUMMIT EVEREST.

. . .

AS SHE CRAWLED ALONG A THIN ICY RIDGE TO THE SUMMIT OF EVEREST,
HER UPPER BODY WAS ON THE CHINESE SIDE AND HER LOWER BODY WAS ON THE NEPALESE SIDE OF THE MOUNTAIN.

I n May 1975, Junko Tabei and her team of fourteen women set out to climb the highest mountain on Earth. One night while they were sleeping, an avalanche buried four members of the team, including Junko. Luckily, their mountain guides pulled them to safety. The team continued on, facing harsh conditions. Twelve days later, Junko made history when she became the first woman ever to reach the top of Mount Everest.

Junko's love of mountain climbing began at age ten while on a classroom expedition. She hoped to continue climbing but was told that this was not a sport for girls. She was considered weak and frail, and her parents didn't have extra money to pay for an expensive hobby. When she attempted to join climbing clubs, men made fun of her. They even said she was just looking for a husband. Junko knew that one day she would prove them all wrong.

In 1969, Junko formed the very first Ladies Climbing Club in Japan. Their motto was Let's Go On an Expedition by Ourselves. After their first expedition to a mountain called Annapurna III in Nepal and China, they planned to conquer Everest. They began raising funds for the expedition. Many people complained that the women should be home raising children instead of climbing mountains. Fortunately, they found enough people willing to sponsor their trip.

When Junko reached the summit of Everest on May 16, 1975, she felt a huge sense of relief and gratitude. This accomplishment became a symbol for women's equality in Japan. Junko immediately set to work on her next goal. In 1992, she became the first woman in history to climb the highest summit on each of the seven continents. Then she set out to reach the highest peak in each country. She managed to complete seventy peaks on her list.

While climbing, Junko saw just how much garbage people left behind on mountains. This garbage affected not only the land but also the people living in mountain communities. Junko went back to school to get her degree. She became an environmental advocate. Not long after, she took a job as the director of the Himalayan Adventure Trust of Japan. She helped build an incinerator to burn garbage on mountains and led "clean-up" climbs. Every step Junko took throughout her life was a step toward women's equality and environmental awareness.

ELANA MEYERS TAYLOR

SPEED-DEFYING BOBSLEDDER, BORN 1984

AMAZING FACTS AND UNBELIEVABLE STATS

ELANA'S OLYMPIC TRAINING SCHEDULE **INCLUDED SPRINTS, SKIPS, AND HEAVY WEIGHTLIFTING.**

. . .

IN THE 2014 OLYMPICS, SHE WAS **A TENTH OF A SECOND AWAY** FROM WINNING THE GOLD MEDAL.

. . .

AFTER A CONCUSSION THAT **ALMOST ENDED HER CAREER,** ELANA PLEDGED TO DONATE HER BRAIN TO RESEARCH WHEN SHE DIES.

. . .

WHEN WOMEN WERE FINALLY ALLOWED TO DRIVE IN FOUR-PERSON SLEDS WITH MEN, ELANA HAD A HARD TIME FINDING MEN WHO WOULD PUSH FOR HER.

When Elana Meyers Taylor was nine years old, she dreamed of becoming an Olympic softball player. Little did she know that one day she would get her wish. Only, she wouldn't exactly be competing on the US softball team. Instead, she would qualify for bobsledding.

In college, Elana played shortstop and pitcher for her softball team. She began training for the Olympics but didn't make the cut. One day, her parents showed her a bobsledding video. Elana was hooked. She contacted bobsledding coaches and was invited to try out.

Bobsledding is an intense sport. Elana looks danger in the face every day. Her sled goes ninety miles per hour, so speed, power, and the ability to make quick decisions are key. If Elana is off by even an inch, the results can be deadly. The only way Elana can succeed in this sport is to trust her intuition and believe in herself.

Elana's Olympic hopes finally came true in 2010 when she won the bronze medal as a push athlete. A push athlete helps push the bobsled to top speeds before the team hops in. Then they try to hold on to their momentum as they steer around dangerous curves. At the 2014 Olympics, Elana took the silver, this time as a pilot. The following year, she became the World Cup champion. In 2018, she won Olympic silver again! She has also collected eight World Championship medals.

Elana is one of the best female bobsledders around, but she's frustrated that women don't have as many opportunities to participate in the sport as men do. Now she's paving the way for women to compete in four-person sledding, an event that used to be open only to men. She and bobsledder Kaillie Humphries made history when they became the first women to drive a four-person sled in the World Cup.

Elana joined a campaign called "Thank you, Mom," to promote compassion, support, and teamwork. She's also joined up with Classroom Champions, a program that connects kids in need with mentors. In 2019, she became the president of the Women's Sports Foundation. This bobsledding pioneer continues to find ways to provide equal opportunities for women and girls while inspiring them to unleash their inner athlete.

DARA TORRES

EXCEPTIONAL FREESTYLE SWIMMER, BORN 1967

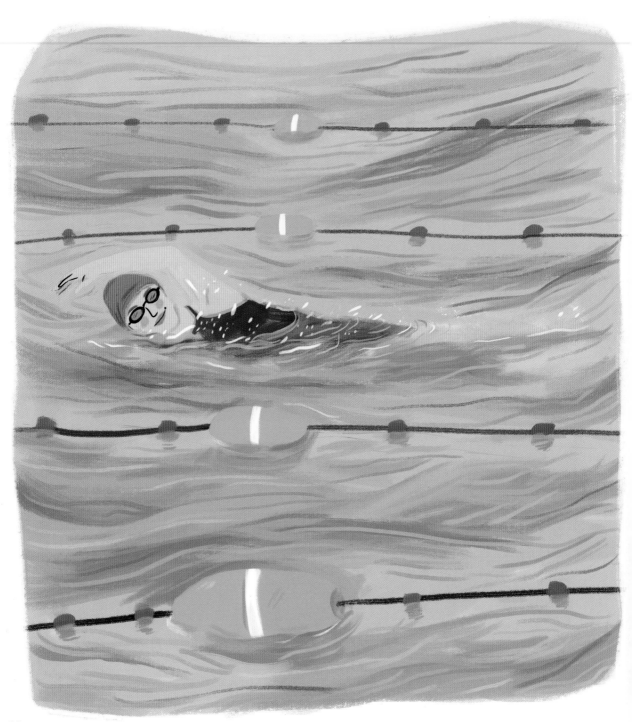

AMAGING FACTS AND UNBELIEVABLE STATS

DARA'S OLYMPIC MEDALS INCLUDE FOUR GOLD, FOUR SILVER, AND FOUR BRONZE.

...

SHE WROTE A BOOK CALLED

AGE IS JUST A NUMBER: ACHIEVE YOUR DREAMS AT ANY STAGE IN YOUR LIFE.

...

ONE OF HER FAVORITE WAYS **TO STAY FIT IS BOXING.**

...

SHE IS THE ONLY SWIMMER TO REPRESENT THE UNITED STATES **IN FIVE OLYMPIC GAMES.**

Dara Torres is the fastest female swimmer in the United States. She won twelve Olympic medals throughout her career, and at the age of forty-one, she became the oldest swimmer on an Olympic team in history. This amazing accomplishment earned her the nickname the Comeback Queen.

Dara began swimming at the age of seven at her local YMCA. Soon she was entering swim competitions. By fourteen, she broke the 50-meter freestyle world record. At seventeen, she won her first Olympic gold on the 4x100-meter freestyle relay. The following year, she accepted a scholarship to the University of Florida and earned twenty-eight All-American swimming honors. She then went on to win even more Olympic medals in 1988 and 1992.

After her 1992 win, Dara took a break from swimming. She moved to New York and found a job in television. But swimming was her passion. She began training for the 2000 Olympic Games. She won five medals, earning her the title of Most Decorated Female Athlete at the Olympics. Not long after that, Dara decided it was time to retire. But it wouldn't be for long.

Five years later, while pregnant with her daughter, Dara was back in the pool. A year after her daughter was born, she broke her own record for the 50-meter freestyle for the tenth time! In 2008, she once again qualified for the US Olympic swim team. She won three silver medals, missing the gold by 1/100th of a second. It was heartbreaking, but it made her fans love her even more. The following year, *Sports Illustrated* named her one of the top female athletes of the decade. She tried out for the 2012 Olympics but missed out by 0.09 seconds. Now officially retired, Dara holds the record for the longest Olympic swimming career—twenty-four years!

Dara speaks about the power of motivation and perseverance and is a spokesperson for SwimToday. This is a program that motivates kids to take up swimming to exercise their mind and their body. She also writes about eating healthy and staying fit. But most importantly, Dara encourages others to pursue their goals no matter how old they are. Her motto is Age Is Just a Number.

MARIANNE VOS

OUTSTANDING CYCLIST, BORN 1987

AMAZING FACTS AND UNBELIEVABLE STATS

WOMEN CAN'T COMPETE IN THE TOUR DE FRANCE,
THE MOST FAMOUS BIKE RACE IN THE WORLD.
SO, MARIANNE HELPED CREATE LA COURSE
BY LE TOUR DE FRANCE JUST FOR WOMEN.
**THEN, SHE WON IT TWICE
—IN 2014 AND 2019!**

...

IN 2017, SHE BROKE HER COLLARBONE
WHEN SHE WAS THROWN INTO A METAL
BARRIER DURING A RACE. ANOTHER RIDER
HAD LOST CONTROL, CAUSING A PILE UP.

...

**IN ROAD BIKE RACING, A PACK OF
RIDERS IS KNOWN AS THE *PELOTON*.**
THEY RIDE CLOSE TO ONE ANOTHER TO SAVE
ENERGY BY REDUCING WIND RESISTANCE.

Marianne Vos took her position on her road bike and waited for the flag to drop. She was about to compete in an eighty-seven-mile race in the 2012 London Olympics. Pouring rain drenched the riders. Soon the race was down to four competitors. In the final sprint, Marianne could hear the roar of the crowd as she crossed the finish line. She had just won the gold by the length of a bicycle. For Marianne, it was the highlight of her career. But she wasn't done yet. That year, she won the Road World Championships, the Road World Cup, and many others. No one was as good as Marianne. This superstar athlete has won over three hundred races in road, track, mountain, and cyclo-cross racing. Oh, and she also holds twelve World titles.

When Marianne was six years old, she watched her brother Anton compete in bike races. She wanted to race, too. She was strong and fast and had a natural talent. Marianne's wish came true when she entered her first race at age eight. By eighteen, Marianne had won the World Championship in cyclo-cross. A year later, she won another World Championship for road racing. In the 2008 Olympics she won gold in the Points Race. *Outside Magazine* named her the world's best bike racer.

But then everything changed. In 2015, after almost ten years of dominating the sport, Marianne began losing. Suddenly, her body wasn't working the way it was supposed to. She needed to rest, so she took six months off to recover. Stepping away from racing made her understand that being vulnerable isn't a weakness, and she learned how to accept herself for who she is.

Marianne began spending her time advocating for gender equality. She is leading the way to expand women's international road racing. Her goal is to make sure that men and women have equal pay and equal race time. One way she is doing this is by getting more people interested in women's racing. She has also started a nonprofit to connect amateur and professional riders. And she has launched Strongher, an online community for women cyclists. Marianne is back on her wheels. She rides not only for herself but for all women who love the thrill of racing.

ABBY WAMBACH

LEGENDARY SOCCER STAR, BORN 1980

AMANZING FACTS AND UNBELIEVABLE STATS

IN 2011, ABBY SCORED HER THIRTEENTH
WORLD CUP GOAL, BECOMING THE
ALL-TIME LEADING
US WOMEN'S WORLD CUP SCORER.

...

IN 2013, SHE BROKE MIA HAMM'S
ALL-TIME INTERNATIONAL
GOAL-SCORING RECORD.

...

ABBY'S YOUNG ADULT MEMOIR IS
CALLED *FORWARD*.

...

SHE HAD TEN HAT TRICKS IN COLLEGE.
A HAT TRICK IS WHEN A PLAYER SCORES
THREE GOALS IN ONE GAME.

Abby Wambach could hear the cheers from the stadium swell into a wave. Brazil scored another goal. The US women's soccer team was losing hope. It was the 2011 quarterfinals of the World Cup, and the Americans were the underdogs. If they lost this game, it would be the earliest US team exit from the World Cup on record. Abby took her position as forward. It was all up to her. She whispered, "Don't miss," then leaped in the air and slammed the ball with her head. She scored the latest goal ever in the World Cup, making soccer history! The game ended on a round of penalty kicks. The final score: USA 5, Brazil 3.

Abby began playing soccer as a kid, often on the boys' teams. She scored 142 goals in high school and ended her college career with a record-setting 96 goals. In 2001, she joined the US national team. The following year, she played alongside famous soccer player Mia Hamm with the Washington Freedom. She was set to score the hundredth goal of her career at the 2008 Olympics. Unfortunately, she fractured her leg just before the Games. A year after her injury, she reached her hundredth goal milestone when she scored against Canada.

Throughout her fifteen-year soccer career, Abby scored more international goals than any other player, male or female—184 to be exact. She held that record for six and a half years until Canadian player Christina Sinclair broke it in 2020. Abby also took home Olympic gold twice, won the FIFA Women's World Cup, and has been named US Soccer Athlete of the Year six times.

But Abby is not *just* a soccer player. She has dedicated her life to fighting for the rights of women. She wants them to be taken seriously and to be paid the same amount as men, especially because the US women's soccer team plays and wins more games than the men's!

In 2015, after her team defeated Japan in the World Cup, Abby retired. She continues to speak out about inequality and the gender wage gap. After giving a graduation speech that went viral in 2018, Abby cofounded Wolfpack Endeavor. This is an organization that helps women develop leadership skills. Her message is: "If we keep playing by the Old Rules, we will never change the game. Welcome to the New Rules."

MARIA
TOORPAKAI WAZIR

COURAGEOUS SQUASH PLAYER, BORN 1990

AMPING FACTS AND UNBELIEVABLE STATS

MARIA WROTE A BOOK ABOUT HER LIFE CALLED
A DIFFERENT KIND OF DAUGHTER: THE GIRL WHO HID FROM THE TALIBAN IN PLAIN SIGHT.

...

SHE HAD TO PRETEND TO BE
A BOY TO PLAY SQUASH, SO SHE USED
THE NAME GENGHIS KAHN.

...

SHE WON THE WILMA RUDOLPH
AWARD FOR COURAGE
FOR OVERCOMING ADVERSITY,
SHOWING EXTRAORDINARY COURAGE,
AND ACTING AS A ROLE MODEL.

...

HER HIGHEST WORLD RANKING
WAS NUMBER FORTY-ONE.

Maria Toorpakai Wazir is a squash player from Waziristan, Pakistan. This remote region is known as one of the most dangerous places on Earth. Most girls there aren't allowed to go to school or play sports.

At four years old, Maria got rid of her dresses, cut her hair, and began wearing her brother's clothes. Her father, an equal rights advocate, allowed her to remain disguised so she could play sports and develop her athletic skills. Bombs often blasted around her as she practiced in her war-torn country.

At twelve, she competed in weightlifting for Pakistan's junior division and ranked second. Soon she switched to squash. When her local squash academy asked for her birth certificate, they found out her true identity. Luckily, the squash director was also a big believer in equality, so he let her play.

Maria began playing squash professionally in 2006 and earned an important award from the president of Pakistan. The following year, the World Squash Federation nominated her for Best Player of the Year. With her success came threats from the Taliban extremist group. They told her to stop playing. The Pakistani National Squash Federation tried to protect her. They offered her security, but it wasn't enough. Soon, it wasn't safe for Maria to leave home.

When it became too dangerous to go outside, Maria practiced in her bedroom. For three years, she wrote to famous squash players everywhere in the hopes they would agree to train her. Jonathon Power, one of the top squash champions in the world, answered her request. In 2011, he brought her to Canada to train. She won many events, including a bronze at the World Junior Championships. Though she remains in Canada, she is still considered Pakistan's number one squash player.

In response to the injustice she suffered, she created the Maria Toorpakai Foundation. This organization helps build peaceful communities and promotes gender equality. The foundation supports education, health care, and sports for young children in remote areas of the world. Maria, who has overcome impossible odds, is spreading the message that hate doesn't solve problems. Now, she dreams of returning to Pakistan to teach other boys and girls squash.

JEN WELTER

**GROUNDBREAKING FOOTBALL PLAYER
AND COACH, BORN 1977**

AMING FACTS & UNBELIEVABLE STATS

JEN'S MOTTO IS KICK GLASS BECAUSE SHE ENCOURAGES WOMEN TO BREAK THROUGH THE "GLASS CEILING." THIS IS A TERM FOR THE BARRIERS WOMEN AND MINORITIES FACE WHEN TRYING TO REACH UPPER-LEVEL POSITIONS.

...

WOMEN MAKE UP HALF OF ALL NFL FANS.

...

HER BOOK IS CALLED *PLAY BIG: LESSONS IN LIVING LIMITLESS FROM THE FIRST WOMAN TO COACH IN THE NFL.*

...

IN 2015, JEN WAS RECOGNIZED AS SPORTS PIONEER OF THE YEAR ON WOMEN'S ENTREPRENEUR DAY.

The day Jen Welter stepped onto the football field as a running back for the Texas Revolution, she became the first woman in history to play a contact position on a men's pro football team. As if that groundbreaking moment wasn't enough, she then went on to become the very first female coach in the National Football League (NFL).

Growing up in Florida, Jen loved playing tackle football with her cousins, but her favorite sport was tennis. When her tennis coach told her that she was too short to play and wasn't strong enough, she switched to soccer. It wasn't until she went to college and joined the rugby team that she learned how to tackle and be tackled.

After graduating, Jen played women's pro football for fourteen years. She mostly played for the Dallas Diamonds, leading them to four championships. She also earned gold medals for Team USA at the Women's World Championship in 2010 and again in 2013. While Jen played football, she continued her education and became a doctor.

Then things really took off. The Texas Revolution invited her to be the only woman on their team. The following year, they asked her to coach linebackers and special teams. At first, the male players didn't take her seriously. That quickly changed when she proved just how much she knew about the game. That season turned out to be the most successful one the Revolution ever had.

The Arizona Cardinals then invited Jen to intern as an assistant coach during their training camp and preseason. This was another huge moment for women in sports. It was the first time a woman had ever coached an NFL team! After coaching for the NFL, Jen became the head coach of the first Australian women's national team. The following year, she signed up as a defensive specialist with the Atlanta Legends.

Now Jen partners with Adidas through the She Breaks Barriers initiative. This program highlights the obstacles that women in sports face. Jen also cohosts flag football camps called GRRRidiron Girls and Camp on the Corner. She even helped design the first-ever women's football cleats. Jen is a role model for every girl who wonders if they're tough enough to play. She knows that if a woman can make it to the NFL, anything is possible.

SERENA WILLIAMS

MEGASTAR TENNIS PLAYER, BORN 1981

AMANZING FACTS AND UNBELIEVABLE STATS

IN 2019, SERENA WAS THE ONLY WOMAN TO MAKE *FORBES MAGAZINE*'S LIST OF

HIGHEST PAID ATHLETES.

...

SERENA AND VENUS FACE OFF AGAINST EACH OTHER ALL THE TIME ON THE COURT, BUT IN REAL LIFE,

THEY'RE BEST FRIENDS.

...

SERENA OWNS HER OWN CLOTHING LINE.

SHE IS ALSO PART OWNER

OF THE MIAMI DOLPHINS FOOTBALL TEAM.

...

THE ONLY PERSON TO HOLD MORE

GRAND SLAM TITLES THAN SERENA IS MARGARET COURT, WHO HAS TWENTY-FOUR.

Fans can't get enough of Serena Williams. Now more than ever, people are watching tennis because of this megastar's powerful moves on and off the court.

Serena began playing tennis at age three. Her father took her and her older sister Venus to play on public tennis courts in California. They lived in a dangerous neighborhood, and the courts were filled with potholes, but that wouldn't slow down these sisters. They had a special talent.

By the time Serena was seven, the family had moved to Florida, and Serena and Venus were training six hours a day. Both sisters became famous, but Serena is a GOAT—the Greatest of All Time. In 1999, she became the second Black woman in history to win a Grand Slam title. (Althea Gibson was the first, way back in 1956.) In 2002, Serena became the number one tennis player in the world, taking three Grand Slam titles. The following year, she won another Grand Slam. The feat became known as "the Serena Slam." That's when a tennis player wins four Grand Slams in a row.

But that's not all Serena has accomplished. This tennis pro has won Wimbledon—the most difficult tournament in the world—seven times. In 2017, at the age of thirty-five, she became the oldest woman to win a Grand Slam Singles title when she beat her sister Venus in the Australian Open. Oh, and she was pregnant at the time! Serena holds a total of twenty-three Grand Slam titles, more than any male tennis player. She has won four Olympic gold medals and holds the record for winning the most women's singles matches in major tournaments.

Serena uses her success to bring awareness to important issues. She and Venus created the Williams Sister Fund to focus on community building. One of their projects was to build a resource center in their hometown of Compton. As one of the few African American tennis pros, Serena discusses the need for equal pay and equal rights. She also talks about body positivity. She wants kids to know that they are beautiful and should be proud of who they are.

KRISTI YAMAGUCHI

INSPIRATIONAL FIGURE SKATER, BORN 1971

AMAGING FACTS & UNBELIEVABLE STATS

KRISTI ADMIRED FAMOUS ICE
SKATER DOROTHY HAMILL SO MUCH,
SHE USED TO CARRY AROUND A DOROTHY HAMILL DOLL.

...

SHE WAS INDUCTED INTO THE
WORLD FIGURE SKATING HALL
OF FAME AND THE US FIGURE
SKATING HALL OF FAME.

...

KRISTI RECEIVED A
THURMAN MUNSON AWARD
FOR EXCELLENCE IN
COMPETITION AND PHILANTHROPY.

...

HER MOTHER WAS BORN IN
A JAPANESE INTERNMENT
CAMP DURING WORLD WAR II,
EVEN THOUGH KRISTI'S GRANDFATHER WAS
A LIEUTENANT IN THE US ARMY AT THE TIME.

Kristi Yamaguchi was born with clubfoot and had to wear casts and special shoes as a child growing up in California. When she was six, her parents encouraged her to take dancing and skating lessons to help strengthen her legs. She readily agreed.

Every morning, Kristi woke up at four a.m. to train with her coach before school. She and her skating partner, Rudy Galindo, won medals in both national and international competitions. In 1988, the two won the pairs title at the World Junior Championship. They continued winning competitions, but Kristi wanted to focus on singles. It wasn't long before Kristi won her first World Championship title.

Kristi's career was just taking off. In 1992, she qualified for the Olympics. Her short program put her in first place as she headed into the free skate. All eyes were on her as she stepped on the ice. She nailed the difficult triple-Lutz triple-toe-loop combination. But then she fell on a triple loop. She kept her cool and finished her routine. No one could predict what would happen next, but the judges agreed: Kristi had delivered an amazing artistic performance. That day, Kristi became the first Asian American to win an Olympic gold medal in the figure skating event. The following year, she won the World Championship for the second time. Kristi had become a role model for millions of kids around the world.

After collecting all those medals, she began skating professionally and toured with the show *Stars on Ice*. Her beautiful performances and her ability to gracefully land difficult combinations drew cheers from the crowds.

Now Kristi is a best-selling children's book author and spends much of her time giving back. She founded the Always Dream Foundation. This is an organization that provides underserved kids with digital books and e-readers. Kristi knows that reading helps people succeed not only in school but in life. As the only Asian American Olympic champion figure skater to date, Kristi continues to inspire on and off the ice.

GET YOUR GAME ON!

The trailblazing athletes you've just read about are fierce, powerful, and play to win. They've broken records, taken risks, and achieved their dreams. Some of them had the support they needed to succeed from a young age. Others had to face almost impossible odds to reach their goals, but they all have one thing in common: They never gave up.

Not only are these athletes the best players in the world, but they've made it their mission to help others. They have spoken out about equality, discrimination, racism, bullying, disability rights, body image, climate change, and more. Their hard work continues to pay off, both on and off the field. Their efforts have helped create new laws, change the rules, and break down barriers.

Hopefully, the athletes in this book have inspired you. Maybe you'll try out for a new team, sign up for ballet lessons, or hit the surf. Maybe one day you'll be a race car driver like Danica Patrick or follow in the footsteps of Marlen Esparza and become the next boxing champion. Maybe you'll climb the highest mountain in the world, like Junko Tabei. You can do whatever you set your mind to.

Like these athletes, you can also be an advocate for change. Start with your community and see where there is a need. Speak up for what's right and fair. You can't do it alone, so ask your friends and family to pitch in. These athletes changed the world, and so can you!

SELECTED SOURCES

Here are some of the books I read to get an in-depth look at the lives of the athletes included in this collection.

Biles, Simone. *Courage to Soar: A Body in Motion, a Life in Balance*. Grand Rapids, MI: Zondervan, 2016.

Buckley, James. *Who Are Venus and Serena Williams?* New York: Penguin Group USA, 2017.

Editors of *Sports Illustrated Kids*. *Women Athletes Who Rule!: The 101 Stars Every Fan Needs to Know*. Des Moines, IA: Sports Illustrated Kids, 2018.

Flanagan, Alice K. *Wilma Rudolph: Athlete and Educator.* Chicago: Ferguson Publishing Company, 2000.

Hinman, Bonnie. *Xtreme Athletes: Danica Patrick*. Greensboro, NC: Morgan Reynolds Publishing, 2007.

Retton, Mary Lou, and Béla Károlyi. *Mary Lou: Creating an Olympic Champion*. New York: McGraw-Hill, 1985.

Schatz, Kate. *Rad American Women A-Z: Rebels, Trailblazers, and Visionaries Who Shaped Our History . . . and Our Future!* San Francisco: City Lights Books, 2015.

Wambach, Abby. *Forward: A Memoir*. New York: Dey Street Books, 2016.

Yamaguchi, Kristi. *Always Dream*. Dallas, TX: Taylor Publishing, 1998.

Zuckerman, Gregory. *Rising Above: Inspiring Women in Sports*. New York: Philomel Books, 2018.

Here are a few fascinating articles about some of the athletes' advocacy work.

CBC News. "Silken Laumann Opens Up About Her Struggles, Wants Canadians to Do the Same." April 9, 2019. https://www.cbc.ca/news/canada/calgary/silken-laumann-website-unsinkable-inspiration-advice-1.5089945. (Accessed September 22, 2020.)

Crawford, Aimee. "Bravo, Simone Biles, for Taking a Stand Against ADHD Stigma." ESPN. September 21, 2016. http://www.espn.com/espnw/voices/article/17602540/bravo-simone-biles-taking-stand-adhd-stigma. (Accessed September 22, 2020.)

DiGiulian, Sasha. "The Importance of Being an Advocate." December 5, 2016. http://sashadigiulian.com/the-importance-of-being-an-advocate. (Accessed September 22, 2020.)

Hariri-Kia, Iman. "How Olympic Athlete Elana Meyers Taylor Got into Bobsledding & Became a Trailblazer in a Male-Dominated Sport." *Bustle*. February, 23, 2018. https://www.bustle.com/p/how-olympic-athlete-elana-meyers-taylor-got-into-bobsledding-became-a-trailblazer-in-a-male-dominated-sport-8227079. (Accessed September 23, 2020.)

Herman, Lily. "7 Seven Ways That Serena Williams Is a Role Model." *Teen Vogue*. August 26, 2016. https://www.teenvogue.com/story/7-ways-serena-williams-is-role-model. (Accessed September 23, 2020.)

Kulp, Miranda. "The Real Fight: How Ronda Rousey Is an Inspiration to All Girls." *Elite Daily*. July 31, 2015. https://www.elitedaily.com/sports/ronda-rousey-inspiration-to-girls/1157364. (Accessed September 23, 2020.)

McGraw, Eliza. "The Kentucky Derby's First Female Jockey Ignored Insults and Boycott Threats. She Just Wanted to Ride." *The Washington Post*. May 4, 2019. https://www.washingtonpost.com/history/2019/05/04/kentucky-derbys-first-female-jockey-ignored-insults-boycott-threats-she-just-wanted-ride/?utm_term=.b5b45abaf5fa. (Accessed September 22, 2020.)

Selby, Daniele. "Soccer Star Abby Wambach Is Fighting to Close the Gender Wage Gap." *Global Citizen*. September 28, 2018. https://www.globalcitizen.org/en/content/abby-wambach-she-is-equal-gender-wage-gap. (Accessed September 22, 2020.)

Tapper, Christina M. "Misty Copeland Is Changing the Way We Think About Ballet Dancers." *Sports Illustrated Kids*. June 29, 2016. https://www.sikids.com/from-the-mag/misty-copeland-changing-way-we-think-about-ballet-dancers. (Accessed September 23, 2020.)

Finally, did you know that it can take up to eighteen months to write and publish a book? That means that while this book went to press, some of these athletes continued to score big! For the most up-to-date stats on amazing athletes who continue to crush it, check out their websites or go to www.Olympic.org.

ACKNOWLEDGMENTS

An author needs a lot of people in her corner to write a book, and I couldn't have done it without the help of my own standout team. Susan Cohen, agent extraordinaire, believed in this project from the kickoff. Nora Long made a great assist. Super editors Allison Cohen, Julie Maytsik, and Amber Morris, along with Marissa Raybuck and the rest of the RP Kids lineup, took it to the next level. Sarah Green's illustrations hit it out of the park. Gregory Payan, Alexander Weintraub, and Lois Weintraub went the distance, making sure I had my bases covered. Kerrie Baldwin, Ed Serken, Blair Glaser, and the SUNY Ulster crew continue to be my own personal cheer squad. Heidi Garnett, Wanda Sherman, and Rise Finkle are always there for both the wins and the losses, usually with really good snacks. Remington, an all-star on and off the field, was the inspiration for this book. Christopher champions my work and catches all my curveballs. This book wouldn't be possible without the unstoppable athletes who have used their platform to bring positive changes to the world, and of course, I'm grateful to my readers for always encouraging me to step up to the plate.

INDEX